The Positively MAD Guide

the Secrets of
Successful Students

Super Speed Study Skills

Michael Tipper

www.positivelymad.co.uk

Visit the web site for examples of:

- **Mind maps**
- **Details of workshops / training**
- **Details of recommended books**

ISBN: 1 873 942 64 8

Published by Lucky Duck Publishing Ltd.
3 Thorndale Mews, Clifton,
Bristol BS8 2HX, UK

www.luckyduck.co.uk

Commissioning Editor: George Robinson
Designer: Barbara Maines
Proofreader: Sara Perraton
Illustrations by Philippa Drakeford
Printed in the UK by Antony Rowe Ltd, Chippenham, Wiltshire

You are not the first to be doing this you know

This is what students who have already learnt about study skills from Positively MAD say:

"I enjoyed learning how to revise and keep it in my long term memory" - Lucy Browning

"I liked learning how to make revision easier, more fun and to remember it" - Rebecca Pavell

"I liked the ability to learn more in less time and effort" - Michael Collins

"It helped me understand how much potential I have. I liked the amount of learning that took place that was actually fun" - Jason Carter

"It has helped me to think about how to revise better to improve my grades." - Anna Matthews

"I can use it when I am revising. It is practical" - Amy-Ruth Davies

"It has provided me with insights into new ways to learn" - Alan Winney

"Useful for upcoming exams" - Jenny Lye

"It's easy to understand and remember" - Natasha Thomas

"I now know that revising can be made more interesting and it doesn't have to be boring. It was fun and enjoyable and easy to understand. The Mind Map will help me with notes much more and now I feel more confident" - Cerys Lewis

"It showed me that revising can be less complicated and produce more effective results. I found it hard to revise but now I am more confident that I am able to revise" - Jenna Chappel

4

Can you learn how to learn?

A few years ago a young lad left school at 16 to join the Navy as an engineering apprentice. Of course he found the basic training quite hard work because it is supposed to be but the thing that worried him the most was the amount of new information that he would need to learn to help him realise his dream of becoming an engineering officer. He struggled with learning the information and so came to the conclusion that he had a bad memory. It seemed to him that his dream of a naval career was slipping from his grasp.

It is strange how these things happen but just as he was beginning to despair, he noticed an advert in a newspaper about a course to improve your memory. He was astounded to see such a thing advertised as he thought that your mental abilities were fixed from birth. Out of curiosity he purchased the course and to his surprise he discovered that it was very easy to train your memory to remember absolutely anything.

He applied some of his new found skills to his naval education and training and quickly started to pass his exams with ease. Now you would think that with this success he would continue to use the techniques but once his early examinations were over he soon "forgot" about the skills that had worked so well for him. Time passed on and he was selected for a commission and then he completed a degree in engineering, amazingly without using the ideas he had used when he first joined up. He found the learning a bit of a slog and although he got quite good marks at the back of his mind he new that there was an easier and better way for him to learn.

An avid reader, our fledgling naval officer developed a voracious appetite for information about how to learn and remember and once again rekindled his interest in the techniques he had originally discovered in his teenage years. Very quickly he realised that he had been a fool because he could have applied some very simple techniques to his studies that would have meant much better results with far less effort in a shorter time (meaning he could have spent more time going out and having fun!). But it wasn't too late to start so he began applying the learning strategies to his specialist submarine training and soon found that they worked very well. His career took off and he became a very successful submarine engineer officer.

As the years passed by he started to realise that his calling lay not in engineering but in teaching what he had discovered about learning to others. Time and time again he kept thinking, "if only I had learnt how to learn when I was at school". One thought particularly bothered him and that was "what if there is a student out there who is struggling with their learning and think it is because they have a problem and not because they just don't know how to learn?" These thoughts compelled him to start teaching others how to learn, a skill that didn't appear to be taught in the school system.

Now one of the problems people have when they change career is that when they begin a new vocation, credibility in the new field needs to be established from scratch. Our naval chap decided that the best way to convince people that they should listen to him was to show them exactly what the mind was capable of by demonstrating it himself. He decided to enter the World Memory Championships.

This annual competition attracts people from all over the world to compete in 10 mentally gruelling events that include amongst other things memorising a number hundreds of digits long, as many packs of playing cards as possible in an hour, a single pack of cards as quick as possible, lists of words and a complete poem. He calculated that it would need at least 6 months of training to achieve a good result in such a prestigious competition and so he set about training his memory.

Sadly as his training was beginning, his mother was taken seriously ill with a brain tumour and over the next couple of months he sat by her bedside as her condition slowly deteriorated and then eventually she passed away. As you can imagine, he was devastated. During her illness he had stopped training for the memory championships and after his mother's funeral had less than 7 weeks left to prepare. He considered abandoning his attempts but kept thinking about how proud his mother had been of his achievements and so decided that he would give it his best shot in her honour.

Over the next few weeks he got up at 5.00am every morning and practised before he went to work. He went running each lunchtime and in the evening did 3 or 4 hours more memory practice. What had become an idea to help gain credibility in a new career now became a quest to honour his mother's memory with an achievement he knew she would be proud of. It was hard work but persistence, self-belief and determination to achieve his goal kept him going.

This effort paid off because he competed in the World Championships and came second winning the Silver medal and becoming a Grand Master of Memory – the highest and hardest to achieve official recognition given to competitors in the championships. He has now left the navy and shares his knowledge all over the world with people keen to use more of their brain's potential.

Why do I tell you all of this? Well the young lad who joined the navy at 16 was me and that was part of my story. I tell it to you because I want to share with you my background. You see when I was at school I thought I had a bad memory. What I didn't know or appreciate was that learning can be easy and it can be fun. What I want you to know is that is true for you too. This manual has been written and designed so that you can learn that learning can be interesting and enjoyable.

WARNING!

This book could seriously improve your life.

So…

Make sure you put your name on this dotted line

....

And be sure to log on to www.positivelymad.co.uk

Why?

Because this book and this website can help to turn you into the seriously successful student you could be for less effort and in less time than you may already be spending being less successful than you should be. That's why.

How?

Because we know the secret of how to become smarter faster, and we want to pass this on to you...

Why?

Because your success is our success. Because success is the name of the game we play.

You give us your attention today, we'll turn you into an Exambuster tomorrow.

How?

Easy. That's the point. What you may never have realised before is that learning is easy.

Modern brain research has proved scientifically that you learn more when you're having fun. And having fun is easy, right? So, what we're going to do today is to learn how to enjoy learning!

Motivation

Try this exercise. Close your eyes and imagine that you're holding a lemon in your hand. Lift it slowly up to the level of your nose and smell it. Now bite into it. Imagine your teeth going through the rind and the juice of the lemon entering your mouth,. Really feel it…

Nice? Chances are that some of you felt your mouth and jaws tingle just as though you had bitten into a real lemon.

So what does that prove? It proves that

your nervous system can't tell the difference between a real and a vividly imagined event.

That's why we feel real fear when watching a horror film, or have real adrenaline flowing through our veins when watching a thriller. It's also why many successful people achieve success. They imagine success. They imagine it so vividly that it becomes a significant factor in helping them achieve it. You can become whoever you want to become if you can believe in yourself sufficiently. (Think about Madonna. Her story is a perfect example of this truth.) And right now we are interested in your performance as a student soon to take, or already in the process of taking exams. This is the importance of positive thinking. The fact is that

our attitude conditions our performance.

Forget about your ability for the moment. The truth is that most of us have the ability that we need to achieve our aims. What we lack is the ability to use our ability. The name of this kind of ability is confidence. (Think about Madonna again.) You probably think that confidence is something you either have or haven't got. Not so. Confidence can be learned. It begins with your imagination. Most of the top class athletes in the world spend a serious amount of their training imagining a successful performance. They imagine this performance in great detail. It becomes part of their belief in themselves. They call it "mental rehearsal". They try to make their actual performance more and more in accordance with their imagined performance, and research has shown that the more thorough and vivid their "mental rehearsal" the more likely they are to succeed.

An obvious trick? Of course! The best tricks always are! Let's use it. Remember that **attitude conditions performance.** If you go around with the mental image of yourself as a lazy student with no ability who can't do Maths or Science or Geography or French or whatever it is, then guess what kind of outcome you're likely to create...? Here's a great tip from one of the world's most successful people:

"Don't look at the problem.
Look at the solution to the problem"

See yourself as a gifted, enthusiastic student, tackling your studies with confident enthusiasm. learning the study skills we're going to teach you today. Imagine how good you'll feel when the results come through the letterbox. You can actually effect reality in this way. Make it real. Once you start thinking this way you'll have real motivation and motivation gives you motor-vation. You can really move...

Successful people are motivated people

At the moment, you are in a learning environment whether it's school, college or even university.   You have a staggering amount of learning to do and during the year you will have to take some examinations. Some people find learning very difficult, the lucky few seem to cope with ease but the majority of us get by muddling our way through the process. We manage to pass our examinations but the learning process seems to be one of gathering lots of notes to gather dust in a folder followed by a flurry of activity just before exam time. That can be quite a stressful process and it certainly isn't fun.

This is because we don't know what we're doing. We are lucky enough to have teachers who know and understand the subjects we need to know and understand, and with work we can learn the information they pass on to us. But we don't usually do this very effectively because

we don't know how we learn.

That makes learning difficult. Most of us sit and read over our notes for long periods of time thinking that in this way we will get the information into our heads and remember it. In fact, under such unpleasant conditions most of us find it almost impossible to concentrate and spend fifty minutes in every hour day dreaming about what we're going to be doing after we've done our "learning".

Spending sixty minutes working, to learn for only ten of those minutes may be what most of you are doing now.

If you follow the games we're going to play today, you'll be spending only twenty minutes working, but you'll also be doing twenty minutes learning.

In other words you'll

learn twice as much in less than half the time!

Good game?

Then let's play!

First however, check your motivation.

Ask yourself...

W. I. I. F. M?

What's in it for me?

What's in it for me?

What are you going to get from learning how to learn? What actual difference is it going to make in your life? As an exercise now, imagine that someone has waved a magic wand and all of a sudden you have the skills and techniques to learn anything that you want to. What impact would that have on your life right now? Use this space to write your answers.

Now think one year into the future and think what your life would be like after having skills and techniques to learn anything that you want, for a whole year. Be precise. It's necessary to use your imagination in a very specific way. What sort of results would you have got, how would you feel about yourself? What would you have done with the extra time you found yourself with? Use this space to write your answers.

Now project your mind even further into the future and see yourself in 5 years time after having had these skills and techniques. What will you be doing with your life then, that perhaps without this knowledge you may not be doing? Really stretch your imagination and visualise and feel what it would be like. Use this space to write your answers.

If you have written down powerful and compelling reasons and vividly imagined what it would be like to have effective learning skills and techniques and the impact that they would have in your life, then you will now have created your own mental rehearsal.

Thinking

From what was said above about motivation, you'll know that

we think in pictures.

Forget about eating lemons. Instead, close your eyes for a few moments and think about your day so far since you got out of bed. Remember what you did before you left your home, what did you have to eat, did you hear anything interesting on the radio? What can you remember about your journey to wherever you are sat right now?

It is likely that you will be able to remember quite a bit of what you have experienced so far today. But which of these statements is true:

1. I recalled everything I had done today as though by reading a type written script in my mind that described everything that had happened to me right to the very last detail.

2. I recalled everything I had done today by seeing images and pictures in my mind.

Of course it is number 2. When we think we do so in pictures. There is the old saying "a picture speaks a thousand words" and if you think about it, that is true. If you were to take a photograph of your surroundings right now, you would capture a tremendous amount of information. BUT, if you were to try and describe the same scene using words alone it would take thousands of words and many pages to capture the same amount of detail.

So knowing that we think in pictures, we may wish to consider using them when we learn

From books and teachers you get information. The trick is to turn that information into knowledge. The way to do that is to visualise the information.

We'll be doing some exercises based on that today but before leaving words for pictures however, we should notice...

The Power of Key Words

Communication through the written word is one of the most effective ways of expressing information, but it is not necessarily the best way of learning it. Studies have shown that about 10% of the words in a text are useful; information carrying words and the rest are there to hold the key words together. So rather than writing down pages and pages of notes, if you identify key words and understand what they mean you will be operating more efficiently. And if you think about it, it is far less work to learn 3 pages of key words than 30 pages of written notes.

Now I would like you to read the previous paragraph again and write down no more that 9 key words that you think are important in that passage. Write them in the space provided. When you have done that, compare your words with the ones I have chosen at the back of the manual.

*   *

*   *

*   *

*   *

*

Meanwhile, since it's your brain that does the learning, it's useful to know how it works! Some of you will be familiar with the discovery of...

Right and left brain thinking..

Your brain is divided in half!!!

The upper part of our brain is divided into two halves. In most people, the left half deals with logic, words, lists, number, linearity, and analysis etc. The right half deals with rhythm, imagination, colour, day-dreaming, spatial awareness, Gestalt (whole picture) and dimension. Studies have shown that the more we use both sides of our brain, then the more effective our overall performance is. "Great minds think alike" in the sense that they use both sides of their brains.

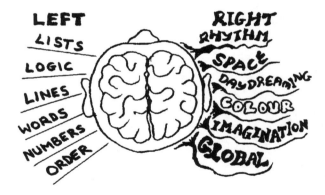

Consider these different functions of the brain and ask yourself which ones you use most often. You'll use all of them to some degree, but you'll use those on one side of the brain a great deal more than others. Just as some people are right handed and others left handed, so too some of us are predominantly left or right brained. If you find you use both sides equally then BRILLIANT because that is what the great minds of our times (eg Leonardo Da Vinci and Einstein) do – they use BOTH SIDES OF THEIR BRAINS. Studies have shown that if you use both sides of your brain then you will learn things much quicker and

remember them for much longer. We will show you how to do this later.

Numbers exercises

On the next two pages there are a series of numbers from 1-40.

Numbers Exercise Part 1

Take a stopwatch and time yourself how long it takes for you to find each number in turn from 1 through to 40 starting at 1, then 2 then 3 and so on. Mark each number with a pen or pencil and remember to make a note of how long it took you when you have found number 40.

When you have done this turn to the back of the book, Appendix 2, and follow the instructions.

Numbers Exercise Part 2

Repeat the process and make a note of how long it took you the second time.

Since we want to turn information into knowledge, then we need to realise that...

information is easier to understand if we know how it is structured and organised.

Which was quicker, the first time you went through the numbers or the second? Of course it was easier to find the numbers in order the second time round once you knew the "secret". Initially you were faced with what appeared to be a meaningless mass of numbers and struggled to find your way through them (or understand them). Once you knew how these numbers were structured or organised it became much easier to navigate or understand them.

18

17   37   18   26

9
                                    2   14
        5   34
25   1
33   38

                        10
                              30
                                        6
        29   13
21
                    22

8   3   31
    12

            27
24
        32
16   40   11   35
            19
                                    39
28
    20   7
    36   15   23
4

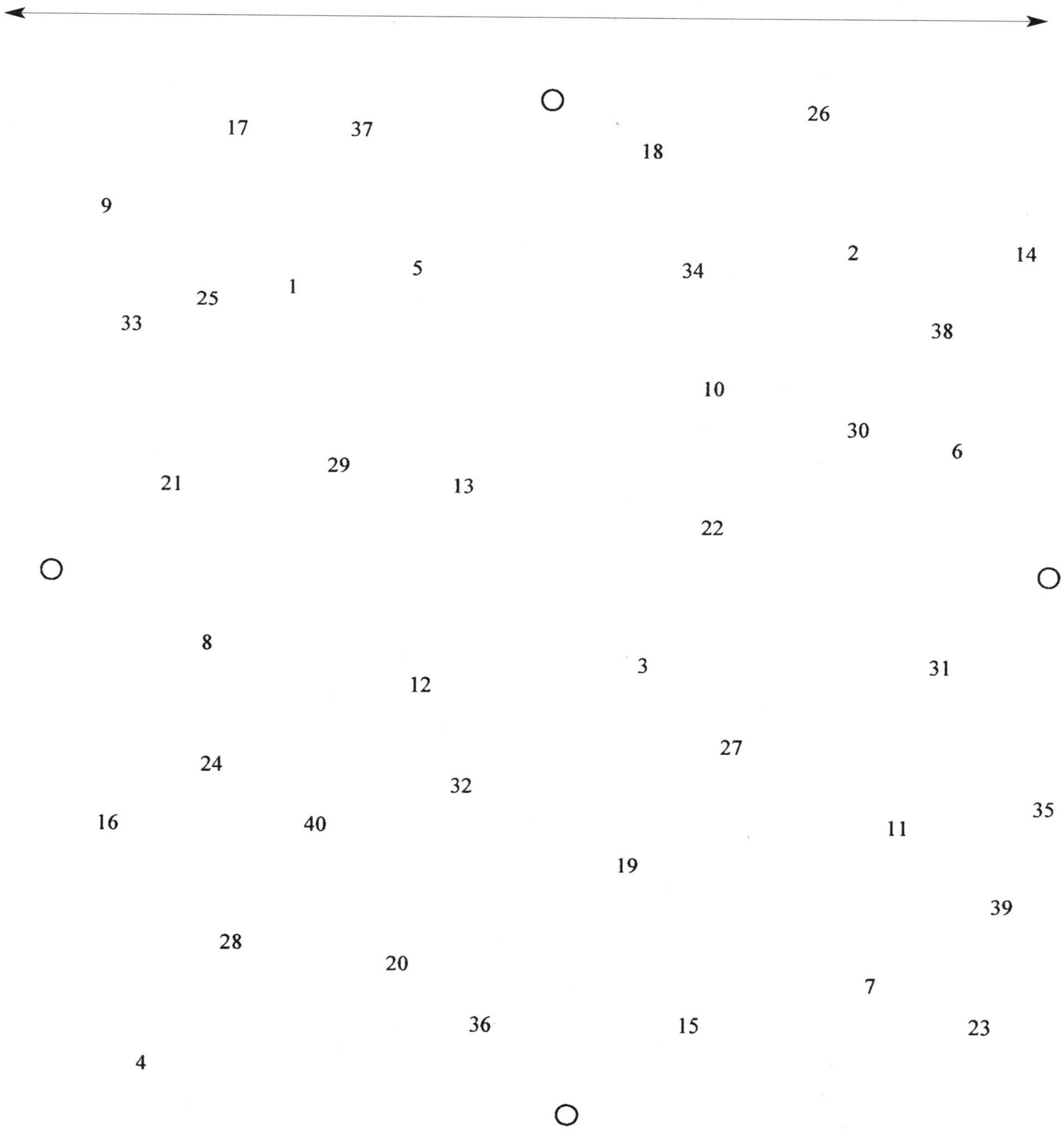

19

17 37 ◯ 26
        18

9

        2   14
5   34
1
25
33   38

10

30
21 29   6
13
22

◯   ◯

8
3   31
12

27
24
32
16 40   35
11
19

39

28
20
7
36 15 23
4

◯

Before we go any further it would be useful to understand the structure and organisation of

Your Memory's

Natural Rhythms

There are a variety of memory techniques that obviously require some conscious effort but we can utilise the mind's natural processes for learning information.

If I were to read out a list of 30 or so words to you and then asked you to recall them for me, you would be able to recall some words from the beginning of the list, some from the end but only a few from the middle of the list. If you don't believe me, try it using the following list of words:

1. Read the list of words to yourself just once.

2. Then turn to the back of the book and go to Appendix 3. Try and recall as many of the words as you can without looking at them again.

> book
> the
> table
> and
> rode
> and
> went
> boxing
> ring
> glove
> punch

went

of

Alexander the Great

and

went

stair

and

light

of

note

paper

light

went

himself

home

time

octopus

These effects are known as **PRIMACY** (words from the beginning of the list) and **RECENCY** (words from the end of the list). Unless you were applying a mnemonic technique (mnemonic means "relating to memory"), it is highly unlikely that you would recall all of the words.

You would however be able to recall words that were **REPEATED** (and, went, of) or **LINKED** (boxing, ring, glove) in any way and any **OUTSTANDING** (Alexander the Great) or unusual words (for example the word "Rhinoceros" in a list of underwear is outstanding just as the word "Underpants" sticks out in a list of large African Herbivores).

You would also remember any that you could **ASSOCIATE** with. See these effects on a graph.

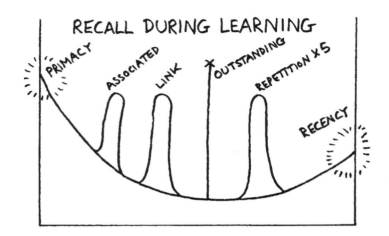

RECALL DURING LEARNING

PRIMACY · ASSOCIATED · LINK · OUTSTANDING · REPETITION x5 · RECENCY

So by looking at this graph we will remember more from the beginning (PRIMACY) and more from the end (RECENCY) but there will be a dip in the middle. Things will also stand out along this curve and they will be the things that you are especially interested in (ASSOCIATED), the things that are LINKED together in some way, anything that a by its very nature is especially unique (OUTSTANDING) and anything that appears more than once or twice (REPEATED)

"But..."

I hear you ask,

"how can we use this?"

Well it is quite simple. All we need to do to remember stuff is to ASSOCIATE the new information to stuff we already know, LINK things together, make it as OUTSTANDING as possible and REPEAT it at least 5 times. We will show you how later.

But the answer is also that it's all a matter of timing. For instance – if we were to study for hours and hours and hours without a break, then we would find that the dip in recall between the PRIMACY and RECENCY effects would be very big.

On the other hand, if we stopped every 5 minutes for half an hour then we would not give ourselves enough time to get into the flow of learning and we might as well not bother.

So we need to find a balance between these two extremes. You will be pleased to hear that I am going to encourage you to take more breaks when you are studying! Split your study time into 20-50 minute chunks with 10 minute breaks in between when it is important that you relax or do something physical or creative.

In order to achieve more we should do less!

TAKE MORE BREAKS

The time chunks will mean that you create more PRIMACY / RECENCY high points and so remember more from your studying. The breaks will give your mind a chance to rest from learning and doing something different will actually stimulate it. Instead of poring over your notes solidly for 3 hours, if you split the time up into 50 minute segments, you will actually remember more during your learning periods. Experiment with this yourself to see what works for you but generally you should aim to work for 20-50 minutes and take a 5-10 minute break.

THE POWER OF BREAKS

Recall After Learning

"Brilliant," I hear you exclaim, "but what about being able to recall this information after I have learnt it?"

Good Question!

Can you imagine only having to learn something once and then have the ability to recall it whenever you wanted?

Too good to be true?

Not at all. It requires a little effort but it's perfectly possible. Let's turn it into a fact.

Imagine this...

You go to a class, listen to the teacher, take really good notes and at the end of the lesson throw your notebook into your bag. How much information do you think you would remember by the end of the following day?

A German scientist called Ebbinghaus proved that within 1-2 days, we can only recall about

20%

of what we have learnt! Losing 80% seems quite a waste doesn't it? Especially if you worked hard to get the information into your mind in the first place. The reason for this is because on a daily basis, your mind has so much information to deal with over and above what you are learning, that the precious data you want to keep gets crowded out or confused by everything else.

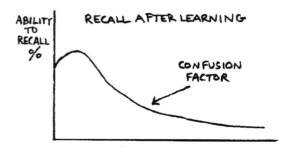

There is a way to overcome that problem. Let's call this technique

" catching the memory at the peak".

This is an easy and quick way to learn what would take you hours and hours of grind to learn otherwise.

The review process

First you need to know that there are several peak moments in your memory system.

1) At the end of an hour's learning, your mind integrates the information that you have just studied so that your ability to recall it actually rises and peaks after about 10 minutes and then falls off dramatically.

2) So, if you review what you have learnt at that 10 minute point, you will reinforce the information at its strongest in your mind.

3) Your ability to recall this information after your 10 minute review will remain at a high point for about a day before it begins to drop off rapidly. So it is a good idea to review what you have learnt again after a day.

4) This second review will mean that your ability to recall what you have learnt will remain for about a week before it begins to tail off again so

5) Review for a third time after a week.

6) After this third review your recall will last for about a month at which time you should do a fourth review which will keep the information accessible by you for up to 6 months.

7) A fifth review after 6 months will mean that the information is firmly logged in your long-term memory. (You may want to put an intermediate review at the 3 month point if you wish just to make sure.)

Review...

after 10 minutes

after a day

after a week

after a month

after 3 and 6 months

If you are worried about all these reviews, don't be because with the right note taking technique (which we will cover later), each review will only take a couple of minutes.

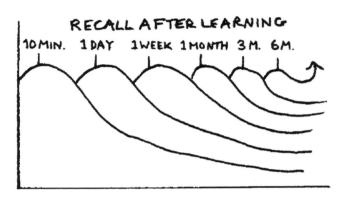

There are two types of review

1. First of all you could just look at the information that you have learnt to remind yourself of its content and relevance to you.

That's fine but a much better way is to

2) Try and recall from memory everything that you learnt (and even everything that you know about the subject)!

Reviewing is an efficient use of time

Sound daunting? If it does then read on...

It need not be daunting. Of course it will involve doing some work, but not half as much as trying to memorise information the traditional way through sheer slog. And it's time well spent. After all, what's the point of spending hours and days and terms working on input (getting the facts into your mind) when you've got no real system to control output (getting the facts back out of your mind)?

Of course all of this reviewing will nevertheless take time and I can hear you telling me that

"its impossible"

to do all that reviewing with the amount of notes you have to take. Well,

that's true

which is why a more effective note taking method is necessary.

Effective note taking

Having covered the power of key words, the importance of combining the left and right brain into our thinking, the use of pictures and the benefit of understanding how information is structured or organised we now need a note taking technique that takes all of this into account. One of the most powerful methods is Mind Mapping®, the technique of making "mental maps" of information.

Mind Mapping

Mind Mapping®

A Mind Map®, invented by Tony Buzan, is an extremely powerful tool. It is a graphical technique that mirrors the way the brain works. The subject of Interest is crystallised in a central image and then the main themes radiate out from the central image on branches. Each branch holds a key image or key word printed on the line. Details are added to the main branches and radiate out. There is extensive use of colour throughout the Mind Map®.

Most people's notes are on lined paper using blue or black ink that looks extremely boring. To make your notes more attractive to your brain, add colour, rhythm and imagination and all of a sudden taking notes becomes much more fun.

Make them interesting

Mind Maps® have a variety of uses including note taking and note making, revision planning, essay planning and problem solving. Of course the beauty of using Mind Maps® is that it combines both left and right brain thinking which means that you will remember the

Uses both sides of the brain

information better than if you just had lines of words.

On the next few pages, you will find the following examples of Mind Maps® and then we will show you how to do your own

Some of the laws of Mind Mapping

A summary of GCSE English Topics

A summary of GCSE Mathematics Topics

Please note that the originals of these Mind Maps are done in colour and they are shown in black and white here for convenience of printing

(The Mind Map is a registered Trade Mark of the Buzan Organisation)

**Visit the website
www.positivelymad.co.uk
for a colour version of
Mind Maps**

Laws of Mind Mapping

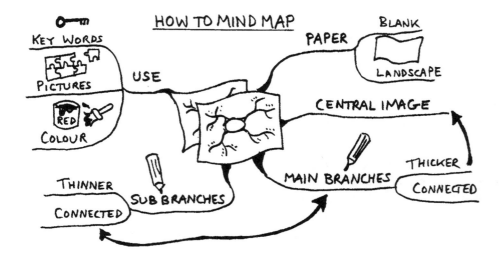

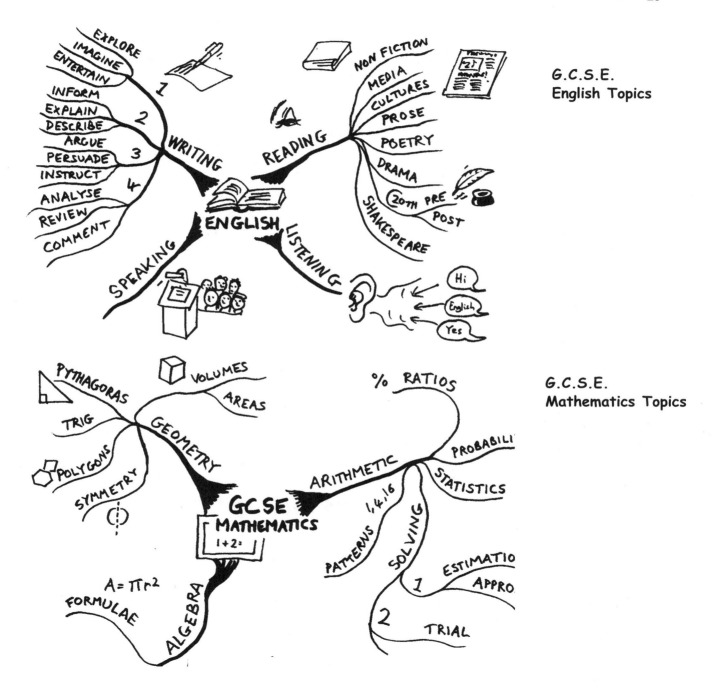

G.C.S.E.
English Topics

G.C.S.E.
Mathematics Topics

How to Draw a Mind Map®

1. Turn your page on its side (landscape), making sure that it is plain paper.

2. Draw your central image using at least 3 colours, making it a picture or symbol that captures the subject of the Mind Map®.

3. Add the main branches that represent the subject's main topics or themes using key words and images.

4. Add the detail on Sub-branches with more key words and images.

5. Use colour throughout and make your Mind Map® as beautiful as possible.

6. Print your words clearly and only use one word per line.

7. Use arrows to connect linking ideas.

Mind Maps can develop in different ways. Either they can grow branch by branch where you fill in all the detail in one section before moving on to the next; or Mind Maps can be drawn level by level where you draw all of the main branches first and then fill in the detail, or a combination of the two. There is no right or wrong way, find out what works best for you.

Your First Mind Map

Now you are going to draw your first Mind Map about the most important person on this planet and that is YOU. Go to one of the blank exercise pages (35 - 38) or get yourself a fresh piece of blank paper.

1. Start by turning your paper landscape

2) Begin drawing your Mind Map about you by starting with a picture or word in the centre of the page that represents you. You could

 or  or **JOHN** or **ME**

draw a sketch of your face, a little stick person, you could write out your name or just write the word "ME".

3) Now add the following main branches to your Mind Map:

FAMILY,
HOME,
SCHOOL,
HOBBIES,
TV, and
FRIENDS.

Now you can
use words:

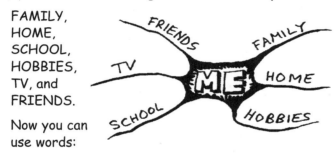

Or you can
use pictures

Or why not a combination of the two approaches – words and pictures?

4) Now add more detail to these branches. So for example: your parents are called Michael and Rabya and you have a brother, Paul aged 6 and a sister, Stefanit aged 14. Your Dad is a manager at a supermarket and your Mum is a nurse. Your gran lives around the corner and visits you every day to have tea with you, your brother and sister. You have a favourite uncle called Faizel and he lives in America. This might look something like this on your Mind Map if you used words:

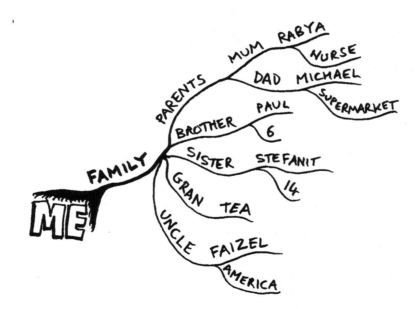

Or like this if you used some pictures too

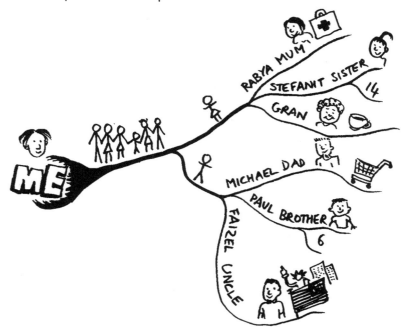

5) Now complete your Mind Map about you by adding more detail to each of the branches. Use the questions below to help you think of things to put on each branch. Remember to use key words and pictures and of course use different colours.

FAMILY – Do you have any brothers or sisters? What are their names and how old are they? Are they still at school or do they have a job? What are your parents' names and what do they do for a living? Do you have a favourite aunt or uncle? Where do they live?

HOME – Where do you live – what town or city? Do you live in the countryside? Do you have a garden? If you have brothers or sisters do you have to share a bedroom with them? What is your favourite room in the house?

HOBBIES – What do you like to do in your spare time? What interests you? Do you play any sports? What are you good at? Are you musical or athletic? Do you support a football or rugby team?

SCHOOL – What school do you attend? What subjects are you studying and do you have a favourite one? Who do you think is your best teacher? What is your favourite thing about going to school?

TV – What do you enjoy watching on Television? What are your favourite programmes? Do you have a favourite soap opera? Do you prefer comedy, drama, music, documentaries or current affairs?

FRIENDS – Who are your friends? Do you have a best friend? What do you like doing together? How old are your friends and what do you like about them?

Do some more Mind Mapping but now you are on your own

The following pages have been left blank so that you can do your own Mind Maps. Why not try one of the following suggestions:

1. Plan your ideal weekend if money were no object and you could do anything you wanted to, where and with whom you wanted.

2) Brainstorm how you could use Mind Maps to help you study.

3) Watch the News on TV and do a Mind Map of what is reported.

4) Prepare the outline for a 10 minute presentation on your hobbies and what interests you.

5) Watch an episode of your favourite soap opera and then use a Mind Map to recall everything that you can remember about what you watched.

Use the following pages to do some of the Mind Map exercises

Use this page to do one of the Mind Map exercises

Use this page to do one of the Mind Map exercises

Use this page to do one of the Mind Map exercises

Use this page to do one of the Mind Map exercises

Reviewing Your Mind Maps

How do you eat an elephant? Of course the answer is one bite at a time. (This has nothing to do with what I'm going to write about, it is just that I've always wanted to include that joke in my writing somewhere!).

It is important to review your Mind Maps on a regular basis to ensure that the information is conditioned in your mind so that you can recall it easily whenever you need to. However, if you are on an intensive course of study, you will find that it is quite easy to become overwhelmed by the ever-increasing number of Mind Maps accumulating in your folders. Having Mind Maps is still going to be a much more efficient way of note taking but even so, how do you keep track of all this information so that you don't let confusion creep in?

One way could be to keep a log of your Mind Maps, together with a record of when to review them. All you would have to do is check the log on a daily basis, see if today's date is in any of the columns and then review that particular Mind Map. An example of what the log might look like, given the review schedule we talked about earlier, would be as follows:

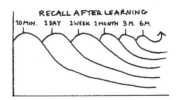

RECALL AFTER LEARNING

Title	Date	Day	Week	Month	3M	6M
English 1	22 Mar	23 Mar	29 Mar	22 Apr	22 Jun	22 Sep
Math 1	22 Mar	23 Mar	29 Mar	22 Apr	22 Jun	22 Sep
Science	23 Mar	24 Mar	30 Mar	23 Apr	23 Jun	23 Sep
Math 2	25 Mar	26 Mar	1 Apr	25 Apr	25 Jun	25 Sep

The time slots are important because they refer to the review cycle we discussed before. Those of you who are organised and like detail will love this method. It does take a bit of discipline but the effort is worth it to make sure that you are not left with 2 weeks of revision to cram into one evening (sound familiar?).

One bite at a time

The Mega Mind Map

Another method of keeping on top of your Mind Maps is to draw a single large Mind Map called a Mega Mind Map that covers your entire topic. So you could have one for Maths, one for Geography and so on. The Mega Mind Map builds up over time as your course progresses. All you do is add the key points from your lessons to it. The beauty of it is that eventually you will see the entire topic on one large piece of paper (use flip chart paper or perhaps the back of a roll of wallpaper or even the back of an old poster) but you will also see it develop and grow. Having this overview will help identify the structure of the subject and the relationships between the various elements of the subject matter. All you need to do is to review the Mega Mind Map once a week for about 20 minutes, reinforcing what you already know and integrating what you have most recently learnt. As you get closer to your examinations, review it more often. This way you don't need to lose what you have learnt in class and it will mean less time studying and more time having fun.

Faced with a completed Mega Mind Map can be quite overwhelming but if you realise that it grew gradually over a number of weeks and months, (one bite at a time?), you can see how a daunting task can be made quite manageable. It really is as simple as that.

The Positively MAD Study Hour

Earlier on in this workbook we covered the power of taking breaks and the importance of conditioning information into our memories so that we never forget it. A great way to do this when you are revising is to use the Positively MAD Study Hour:

Mind Map new material	Break 5 min	Recall old material day / week / month	Break 5 min	Review material covered at start	Break 5 min
20 min		15 min		10 min	

Begin your session by Mind Mapping new material for about 20 minutes. Then take a 5 minute break. Getting up from your desk and going for a brief walk is ideal (remember the power of breaks). After you break spend 5 minutes recalling what you learnt yesterday, 5 minutes recalling what you learnt last week and another 5 minutes recalling what you learnt last month. Then take another 5 minute break before spending 10 minutes recalling (ideally re-drawing your Mind Map from memory) what you learnt in the first 20 minute session of the hour. Then to complete the hour, take another break to get yourself ready to start again.

This is a great way of combining the learning of new information with the consolidation and conditioning of old information already learnt so that you don't waste that time and energy. By taking breaks, you also keep fresh and alert and so if you wanted to, you could do this all day.

This way you can comfortably take in new material and still keep on top of the stuff you have already learnt without getting stressed out.

Memory Skills

The Secret to having a great memory

The secret to a good memory is that we should take what we want to remember, and then using our IMAGINATION make it OUTSTANDING, ASSOCIATE it to something that we already know and CONDITION ITS RECALL until we can't get it wrong.

We will use some key principles to use our imagination to make things outstanding and apply these to a number of techniques to associate them to things we already know and then review them to ensure that we have memorised them.

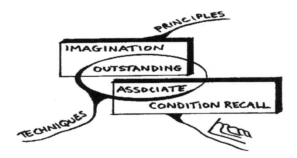

Key Principles of Effective Memory Techniques

1. **Use your senses** - Most of the great natural memorisers blended their senses and introduced the following elements when they memorised:

Vision	Hearing
Sense of smell	Taste
Touch	*Kinaesthesia

   (*awareness of body position/movement).

So the more that you involve your senses, the greater your ability to recall the information that you have learnt.

2. **Include Movement** - The most conspicuous person in a crowded room will be whoever moves the most. Movement helps create links and links are good for memorising information.

3. **Use Exaggeration** - Exaggeration of size, shape and sound will enhance the image. If you saw a 10-foot high mouse wandering around your hometown, I am sure that you would remember it!

4. **Colour** - If we introduce the facilities of both sides of the brain into our memory techniques our overall performance improves - Colour is a feature of the workings of the right side of the brain. Also the more colourful the image, the easier it is to remember.

5. **The more absurd the better** - It is not very often that you see a pink elephant playing the banjo whilst sitting on top of a large, bright yellow Rolls Royce is it? If you saw that I am sure you would remember it for a long time afterwards. The reason is that it is an absurd occurrence and one you would not normally see. If you can visualise absurd images as you memorise and use them to learn information, those images will stick in your mind long term.

6. **Link** - As you create the visual imagery, make sure you link things together with strong and powerful associations.

7. **Humour** - Have fun with your memory and make all of your images funny, absurd and ridiculous. If you watch pedestrians walking past a lamp post in a crowded street nothing really stands out until someone does not watch where they are going and..........

8. **Make your images representative** - A picture speaks a thousand words and so a more meaningful image that represents something boring or abstract will aid the memory process. Quite often your images will have nothing to do with what you are learning but they will trigger the meaning you want to recall.

Let me give you an example of how all these principles can apply to one particular example.

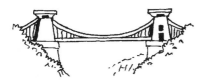

Isambard Kingdom Brunel was a famous engineer and architect in the 19th Century. He was responsible for building bridges, ships and numerous railway lines and stations in England. So how can we remember this?

I want you to imagine a large green pig as big as a house carrying two blue suitcases, running along a station platform trying to get onto a steam train that is starting to leave the station (IKB built railway lines and stations). You can hear the pig's thunderous footsteps as it bounds alongside the train and you are almost deafened as the train's steam whistle goes off right in your ear. Unfortunately for the pig every door has strong steel bars across the opening to the carriage with a sign that says "No Pigs Allowed" and so it can't get on the train. The pig thinks to himself "Is ham barred from this train?" (ISAMBARD) As he makes one final attempt to board the train there is someone inside the door, wearing an ornate shiny crown and a long soft red velvet robe. He is called Dominic (because his large orange name badge stuck to his forehead says so). He looks at the pig and says, "My name is King Dominic and you can't board my train" (KINGDOM). The pig thinks quickly and pulls out from his suitcase an enormous ornate model of a yellow bridge that has the front end of a pink ship sticking out awkwardly from the top and offers it to the king (IKB built bridges and ships) The king says "Well why didn't you show me that before, come aboard", at which point the king opens up the bars and drags the pig onto the train. Quite out of breath the Pig is offered a drink and it asks for a cup of tea. The king brings a pot of tea and says to the pig "I like to help the tea brew by nailing the teapot to the wall" (BRUNEL) at which point he takes a huge hammer from under his royal robe and smashes a 6 foot long nail through the teapot spilling hot tea and bits of broken of china everywhere.

Read this through a few times and really experience the story in your own mind. Now that you have done that, go back to the list of the 8 key principles and see where in the story they have been used.

In the future, if you apply all of the elements above to your mnemonic imagery, then you are on your way to developing a good memory. All that you need now is a mnemonic technique to apply these principles to.

Peg System

Make associations

Association is one of the keys to a good memory. If you leave your coat in a cloakroom at a theatre, you will be given a ticket. When you return you expect to exchange the ticket that you were given for your coat. That is because the ticket you had was associated with the peg that held your coat. The same works with your memory. To remember a list or a sequence of items, simply associate each item to the pegs that you have already created in your mind using the Key Principles described above. When you recall, you simply go to each peg and the association will prompt the information stored.

The Journey Technique

The Journey Technique is a peg system that was used by both the Romans and the Greeks at a time when the ability to recite long passages of texts was a sign of being a great orator. It is also a technique employed by professional memory men. It is a peg system in its own right and utilises locations in or around places that you are familiar with.

Imagine the house where you live, see the front door as you walk in. Then, in your mind's eye, walk through the house visiting every room in turn, just as if you were really doing it. That was quite easy wasn't it? The key to this technique is to pick 10 specific places in your house (individual rooms or specific pieces of furniture) so that as you walk round your house in your imagination, you visit each place in turn in the same order each time. You may have chosen the following:

1. Front Door
2. Table Hallway
3. Sofa in lounge
4. TV in your lounge
5. Kitchen
6. Stairs
7. Bed in bedroom
8. Wardrobe
9. Bath
10. Toilet

In your mind you may have seen something like this:

"*The blue FRONT DOOR opens into a long hallway. Walking past the ornate wooden HALLWAY TABLE, you make your way into the lounge. In the corner of the lounge is your favourite orange SOFA opposite your TELEVISION. At the far end of the lounge is the door to the KITCHEN with its bright white worktops and blue and white tiled floor. In the hallway again you go up the STAIRS to your bedroom and sit on your large wooden framed BED. In the one corner stands your large WARDROBE. Back onto the landing you walk into the bathroom and see the white BATH next to the matching TOILET.*"

Now let's look at a list to memorise:

Tomato

Birdcage

Chair

Pencil

Donkey

Soap

Telephone

Path

Bed

Doughnut

Now using the Key Principles of effective memory techniques, we will associate each item on the list with a stage of the journey. For example, we associate a tomato with the front door, a birdcage with the hall table and so on. So our journey may have looked like this:

"*A large red tomato the size of a football, just thrown against the blue FRONT DOOR knocks the door open revealing the tall red bottomed birdcage on the ornate wooden HALLWAY TABLE which rattles noisily as you bump into it. As you enter the lounge you step back in surprise as someone has placed a massive chair on top of your favourite orange SOFA. You wanted to watch TELEVISION but unfortunately it is not working because of the six-foot long pencil that has been pushed through the screen. You decide to have a drink but you can't get into the KITCHEN because a large donkey is sat on the floor braying loudly. You have had enough, so you decide to go to bed. On your way up the STAIRS you keep slipping over the yellow bar of soap that can be found on each step. You finally make it to the bedroom but cannot get into your BED because a large purple telephone is in the way and is ringing quite loudly. All of a sudden, the WARDROBE door bursts open as two workmen start laying a path across your bedroom floor. You go out onto the landing and into your bathroom only to see a four poster wooden bed sat in your BATH. And if that wasn't bad enough, a huge sugar coated doughnut is in the pan of your TOILET."*

To remember the list, just walk through your journey in your mind and you will see the tomato on the door, the birdcage on the hallway table etc. Now without looking at the story let's see how effortlessly you have memorised this list of associated items:-

What item was connected to the:

Bed ....

Toilet ....

Sofa ....

Front Door ....

Television ....

Bath ....

Stairs ....

Hallway table ....

Wardrobe ....

Kitchen.....................

Where was the :

Chair ....

Path ....

Soap ....

Birdcage ....

Bed ....

Doughnut ....

Tomato.....................

Donkey.....................

Telephone ....

Pencil ....

Quite impressive, considering that there are no connections between these items except for the ones we created in our story. Try memorising a similar list without this technique and see how much longer it takes!

How to use this technique

With this technique you can remember absolutely anything you want to for example speeches, information for exams or any other information that you need to have at your fingertips. It is a very flexible system and its potential, is only limited by the number and length of the journeys that you are able to create in your mind.

Now it's your turn

Now create three of your own journeys by picking places that you know really well such as your home, a friend's house, somewhere in the city, town or village where you live. You may even want to use locations around school or college. Each number in the column represents a distinct location on your journey. Mentally walk along your route to familiarise yourself with it and then pick suitable locations that you can use as pegs. Once you have chosen the 10 locations for each journey, practice visualising the journey both forwards and backwards so that you have a clear and vivid image of each place and that every time you mentally "walk" the journey, the order of the places is always the same.

Journey 1	Journey 2	Journey 3
1	1	1
2	2	2
3	3	3
4	4	4
5	5	5
6	6	6
7	7	7
8	8	8
9	9	9
10	10	10

Now use your journeys to remember the following information by applying the principles that we have already talked about (remember Isambard Kingdom Brunel?):

The first 10 elements of the periodic table	A shopping List	The last 10 US presidents
1 Hydrogen	1 Brown Sliced Bread	1 George W Bush
2 Helium	2 Low Fat Milk	2 Bill Clinton
3 Lithium	3 Stilton Cheese	3 George Bush
4 Beryllium	4 Menthol Toothpaste	4 Ronald Reagan
5 Boron	5 Motoring Magazine	5 Jimmy Carter
6 Carbon	6 Black Pepper	6 Gerald Ford
7 Nitrogen	7 Apple Pie	7 Richard Nixon
8 Oxygen	8 Broccoli Florets	8 Lyndon Johnson
9 Fluorine	9 Cherry Tomatoes	9 John F. Kennedy
10 Neon	10 Spring Onions	10 Dwight D Eisenhower

When you have done this, amaze you friends with your new, amazing memory and then teach them how it is done.

The Linking (or Story) Technique

The linking (or story) technique is a method for remembering a sequence of information such as a list. We are going to use it to remember the order of the planets in our solar system from the Sun, which are:

Mercury, Venus, Earth, Mars, Jupiter, Saturn,

Uranus, Neptune, Pluto.

Make it vivid - remember the eight key principles

Some of you will have noticed that I have left out the asteroid belt. If you want to put it in then please do.

As the name implies, the Linking (or Story) Technique links each item in the form of story. Very simply, the technique relies on making a vivid story that not only helps you remember each of the items, but also the order in which they appear. Consider the following story and as you read on, try and vividly imagine what is being described. It is really very important that you use your imagination to create the story so that it is as real as it could possibly be. Use all of your senses and really enjoy the process.

Imagine a huge ball of glowing orange fire. This of course represents the SUN. Feel the heat coming off this huge orange ball and see the flames dancing around it. Next to this orange ball is a small thermometer (the planet Mercury is a very small planet). As the glowing ball gets hotter and hotter the MERCURY inside the thermometer rises as it expands with the heat. Eventually the Mercury gets so hot that it explodes out of the end of the thermometer with a huge bang and sprays Mercury droplets everywhere.

These Mercury droplets are tiny silver beads of metal that fall on to a beautiful blonde goddess wearing a white toga with a plunging V-neck line. This lady exudes love and compassion because she is the goddess VENUS, the goddess of love. To get away from droplets of Mercury, Venus starts digging a hole in the ground and she does, she piles up a huge mound of brown EARTH. As she digs away furiously the pile of

earth gets bigger and bigger and bigger and suddenly she unearths an angry red faced man eating a MARS Bar (Mars is a small red planet). Outraged, he throws his Mars bar away but it hits a huge muscular fellow who happened to be walking by. Unfortunately for Mars this is JUPITER the King of the gods. As Jupiter walks towards the commotion, on his white T-shirt are the letters S.U.N. that stand for SATURN, URANUS and NEPTUNE. Behind him a little dog that looks just like the cartoon character PLUTO jumps out of his back pocket and trots at his heels.

Now to remember the order of planets all you need to do is recall the story starting at the sun. Imagine the hot sun. What do you see next to the sun? A tube that contains **MERCURY** of course. Who gets covered by the Mercury as it falls? The goddess **VENUS.** What does Venus do to escape from the burning metal? She digs a hole and builds up a pile of **EARTH.** Who does she unearth? The little red faced man (**MARS** is known as the red planet) eating a MARS bar. When he throws the MARS bar, who does it hit? It hits **JUPITER** the king of the gods. What has Jupiter got on his T-shirt? The letters S, U and N which stand for **SATURN, URANUS** and **NEPTUNE.** Who is the little dog that jumps out of the back pocket and follows the chap wearing the T-shirt? The little dog looks just like **PLUTO.**

To really reinforce the story in your mind, you need to review it at least five times over a couple of days. When you review it, you need to vividly experience the story in all its detail. Then, whenever you are asked to recount the order of the planets from the sun, all you need to do is think of the hot orange ball of heat with the thermometer full of MERCURY..........

S.U.N

Review and make it vivid - this technique can be used for any information.

So can you use this for other information? Of course the answer is yes. If you need to learn any factual information, you can create a story to link the items of information together. You could remember a shopping list, or the main themes running through a particular novel or play. You could have the main points concerning a particular answer to an exam question linked in this way. There are really no limits to how you can use this system. You can make your story as long or as short as you like, it is really up to you. Just make it vivid and outstanding and reinforce it at least five times.

1.

2.

3.

4.

5.

6.

7.

8.

Can you remember what the 8 principles of effective memory techniques are to help you do this?

Why not try and make up a story to remember the following information and then test yourself with a friend.

Shopping List

Soap	Wine
Cotton Wool	Potatoes
Tissues	Shampoo
Fishcakes	Peas
Carrots	Yoghurt

Use this space to write your story

The last 10 UK Prime Ministers

Tony Blair

John Major

Margaret Thatcher

James Callaghan

Harold Wilson

Edward Heath

Harold Wilson

Sir Alec Douglas-Home

Harold Macmillan

Sir Anthony Eden

Use this space to write your story

How to Learn Foreign Words

Repetition is boring!

The best way to learn a language is to immerse yourself totally both in the culture and the language itself with native speakers who do not speak your own language. It is the quickest way to learn because that is how we learnt our mother tongue. However it is unlikely that you are going to get the opportunity to do that but however we learn the language, the foundation of our success in the language of our choice will be a good solid vocabulary. Learning new words by repetition can be extremely boring and can be the factor that puts many people off from becoming proficient in a new language. (This is true of other subjects too. Learning by repetition has a limited value but it also has a steep downside because its boring, and boredom does not assist learning. Notice how little repetition there is in our high speed study skills). Learning new words can be easy and fun and there are a couple of ways of doing this.

When you learn new words, quite often their similarity to the equivalent word in your mother tongue will immediately give you the translation. For example if you are English and you are learning German, the word for Boat is Boot. If you are French and you are learning English, the English for lettre is letter.

The similarity may be in the way the word is pronounced (as in Boat/Boot) or it may be in the way the word is spelt (as in lettre/letter).

Boot   Boat

Lettre   Letter

It does not really matter as long as you identify the similarity

and then use it to help you translate.

In German, Hafen means harbour so you could associate Hafen with haven because in rough weather, a harbour is a safe haven for ships. Therefore, another way to remember a foreign word is to

find some sort of relationship

to the English word. Another example is the French translation of carpet, which is tapir. You could use the link with tapestry to remember that translation.

With most words, there is no obvious link to the English translation, so we have to

use our imagination

and create one using mnemonics.

Let us pick a word that we want to remember - I am going to choose Seife which in German means soap. Now when I hear the word Seife, the German pronunciation (sounds like - ZIEFER) is very similar to the word siphon (a plastic tube that opens out at one end into V or U shape). Other words that you could use are cipher, sofa or xylophone.

It does not really matter what the word is

as long as it is the first one that comes to mind for you. In my imagination, I now need to associate an image of a siphon with an image of soap using the principles of a super power memory listed above earlier in the manual.

I imagine an enormous siphon made of clear red plastic rolling around the rim of a bright blue bucket (I hear the sound of plastic rubbing on plastic) into which it has been placed. Another bucket hovers above the siphon and is pouring tonnes and tonnes of white soap powder into it (I hear the hiss of the powder as it falls into the rim of the siphon and see the tumbling stream of white particles). It is important to make the siphon and the soap the dominant images of the picture that I create otherwise I could confuse myself and translate "Seife" into bucket. A hose pipe is pouring gallons of water into the siphon so that loads and loads of soft white soap suds start overflowing from the siphon, engulfing the bucket and everything in the soap's path. I can even taste the soap as it covers everything. Eventually, all that I can see is the white soapsuds and the large red siphon.

It is important to create strong, vivid images

when you form these pictures. Equally important is that I practice the translation in my mind several times so that the link is strong. So when I hear the word Seife I think of siphon and immediately the image comes back to me and I see and taste the soap. So to build up a

Make strong, vivid images

strong vocabulary in your new language, you just create images using the technique I have described above. This process can be applied to nouns, adjectives and verbs. Try the following examples for yourself:

Leiter in German means Ladder (tip - you could feel lighter as you climb the ladder)

Livre in French means Book (tip - open your book and see pieces of liver on each page)

People in Spanish is Gente - pronounced hen'tay (tip - see a crowd of people dipping hens into large cups of tea)

As you will discover when you learn other languages, you will have to consider the gender of the word. In German, nouns can be feminine, masculine or neuter.

There are several ways of learning gender.

For example, if you are male, you could involve yourself somehow in the image of all masculine words by taking part in the scene that you create (likewise if you are female see yourself involved with the image of all feminine words). For feminine words you could also imagine yourself as a spectator watching someone else (a female friend perhaps) taking part in the image. In my image I see a woman holding the siphon because it is a feminine noun. You may wish to include an animal such as a pet dog in every image of a neuter noun

It only takes 30 seconds

To summarise the techniques for translation:

1. Is the translation obvious? If it is you don't need to use a mnemonic technique.

2. Can you find some logical relationship between the word and its translation? If so use that to help your translation.

3. Create a vivid picture relating an image of the English word with an image created by manipulating the foreign word using the principles of a super power memory.

4. Manipulate the image to account for the gender of word by adding specific imagery.

5. Repeat the above for every word you wish to learn.

The process I have described only sounds rather long winded because I have described it at length. Actually it doesn't take long to do. You will find that you will only have to spend 30 seconds at most to create and strengthen your images so that

in an hour you could learn as many as 120 words!

If you did 10 words a day taking only 10 minutes you could learn over

3500 words in a year!

Compare that to the time it takes to learn the same number of words by repetition! It will only work if you try it and put in a bit of short term effort to get long term rewards. It will tax your imagination but it will be worth the effort. An important point to note is that the mnemonic is only a temporary crutch for you to rely on because as you become more proficient in the language (which will only come through continued use), you will "just know" that Seife means soap.

Repetition is boring and inefficient

Can I use this for anything else?

Yes, this process could also be used for unusual, complicated or scientific terms that appear to have no logical meaning. For example the hippocampus is the part of the brain responsible for long term memory. Perhaps you could image a large hippopotamus on a camping trip (see the tents) tying a big knot in his handkerchief so that he can remember where he has pitched his tent! You will of course have to use your imagination, but that can only be a good thing.

Visual/Auditory/Kinaesthetic

We have already said that if we use all our senses when we memorise information then we will remember more. As you know we have 5 senses and the ones that we tend to take most of our information in as we make sense of the world are our vision and what we see, our hearing from the sounds around us and our feelings from what we touch and experience through our emotions. We learn from these 3 senses but not to an equal degree. For example you may prefer to see things written down before you can really grasp it. Or you might

Visual
  Auditory
    Kinesthetic..
What is your preferred mode of learning?

prefer to hear an explanation rather than read it from a book. Others of you may like to take things apart and get stuck in with your hands if you really want to understand something. Whilst we will process information through the senses each of us has a dominant mode of learning. We can enhance our learning significantly if we know what it is and then direct our learning through that particular sense. Certainly, if we combine all of those modes of thinking then we will certainly improve our ability to learn. This is very similar to what we said about left and right brain functions.

Learning by Seeing, Speaking and Doing

It has been discovered that we learn:

10% of what we read
20% of what we hear
30% of what we see
50% of what we see and hear
70% of what we say
90% of what we say and do.

So if we combine all of this we could learn faster. Here is a very quick way of learning to count to ten in Japanese by seeing, speaking and doing. Consider the following (taken from the Learning Revolution by Gordon Dryden and Dr Jeannette Vos):

English	Japanese	Say	Do
one	ichi	Itchy	Scratch your
two	ni	Knee	Knee
three	san	Sun	Point to sky
four	shi	She	Point to girl
five	go	Go	Walk
six	roku	Rock	Rock 'n' Roll
seven	shichi	shi-chi	Double Sneeze
eight	hachi	hat-chi	Put on hat
nine	kyu	Coo	Coo like a dove
ten	ju	Ju	Chew (or don Jewish cap)

If you practise that a few times you will be able to count to ten in Japanese with no problem. So by seeing (having read this page) and then saying and doing, you will have learnt some new information very quickly. What other things can you learn quicker in this fashion?

And Finally…

We have covered a tremendous amount of information about how to learn things more quickly and more effectively and how to retain that information for as long as you want. You now know how to Mind Map®, you have some memory techniques, you know how to improve your reading speed and we have given you some ideas about using your Multiple Intelligences and your senses.

How will you use all of these new found skills? Perhaps you may want to look at what motivates you. Remember the exercise that we did at the start of the book? Have a look at that once more and do the exercise again now that you know what you are capable of.

If you really apply all these skills to your work, you will become outstandingly successful in your studies. For more information on how to develop super speed study skills and other information that can help and support you, check our web site at www.positivelymad.co.uk, or contact us by e-mailing us at info@postivelymad.co.uk

We must also tell you that not only is there much more to learn about this subject, but accelerated learning itself is part of a larger thing, part of a new phenomenon sometimes referred to as the "human potential movement". It's called this because, although everybody has potential, few people have realised their potential to the full. There are many reasons for this, including everything from lack of opportunity and adverse circumstances to negative conditioning and simple lack of "know how."

All these problems can be overcome. (Problems exist in order to generate solutions. That's what problems are for!) Ask yourself this simple question – "Who do I want to be? What kind of person do I want to become?" Now believe this simple answer –

"You can become whoever you want to be, provided you know how, and provided you have the necessary resources".

Part of our mission is to make the necessary resources easily available to people like you and one way that we do that is through the specially selected books in the Positively Mad online bookshop and through other information available on our web site at www.positivelymad.co.uk Think of the ideas that you will find there as being like the tools in a toolbox. Whatever kind of life you decide to design for yourself, these tools will enable you to build your life according to your design. And the tools come with a full set of instructions on how to use them - the "know how". With the know how you will be able to realise your full potential, which is greater than you – or anyone else – ever dreamed.

You are about to embark on the most exciting adventure of the twenty first century. It's called "design your own destiny". So...welcome to the master game... and remember, Positively Mad is dedicated to helping and supporting you on your journey.

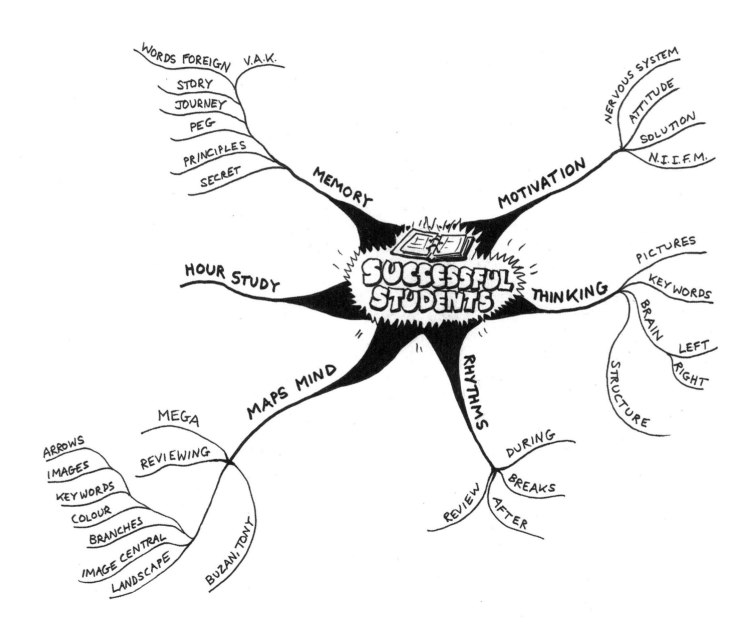

Appendix 1

The Power of Key Words

Remember when we talked about the use of key words? Well you could have chosen the following words:

Communication through the **written** word is one of the most effective ways of expressing information, but it is not necessarily the best way of learning it. Studies have shown that about **10%** of the **words** in a text are **useful**, information carrying words and the rest are there to hold the key words together. So rather than writing down pages and pages of notes, if you identify **key words** and understand what they mean you will be operating more efficiently. And if you think about it, it is far **less work** to learn 3 pages of key words than 30 pages of written notes.

This would leave you with

Communication

Written

10%

Words

Useful

Key Words

Less Work

Now it is important to understand that these are the words that I have chosen that are important to me. Your choice may have been slightly different and there are no right or wrong answers here. The key point to remember is that the key words must summarise FOR YOU what the passage means.

Appendix 2

Numbers Exercise

Now that you have found all forty numbers we will reveal a little secret to you. If you go back to the numbers you will see a small circle at the top and bottom of the page ○ join these with a straight line. You will see similar circles at the middle of the right hand left sides of the page - join these with a straight line. You should now have the numbers divided into four quarters or quadrants by a cross. The "secret" to the numbers is that you will find number 1 in the top left hand quadrant, number 2 in the top right hand quadrant, number 3 in the bottom right hand quadrant, number 4 in the bottom left hand quadrant, number five in the top left hand quadrant and so on working clockwise until you find number 40 in the last quadrant.

Now that you know this, go back to the second page with the numbers on and starting from 1 again, find the numbers from 1-40 in that order and time yourself as you do it.

Appendix 3

Recalling the list of words

Can you remember the list of 28 words on pages 20-21.

OK - prove it by writing down as many as you can on the next page (without looking back). They do not have to be in the same order.

1	2
3	4
5	6
7	8
9	10
11	12
13	14
15	16
17	18
19	20
21	22
23	24
25	26
27	28

Did you remember more from the beginning and the end of the list?

Did you find it harder to recall words from the beginning of the list?

Which words were easier to remember?

Bibliography

Buzan T, 1974, Use Your Head, BBC Books
Buzan T, 1993, The Mind Map Book, BBC Books
Dryden G. and Vos J. 1999, The Learning Revolution, The Learning Web
O'Brien D. 2000, Learn to Remember, Duncan Baird Publishers
Tipper M, 2000, The 77 Habits of Highly Effective Students,
Michael Tipper Publishing

www.positivelymad.co.uk